TABLE OF CONTENTS

Dedication 7

Introduction 8

Family and Friends....................9

Illness and Accidents 10

Your Feelings 11

Saying Good-bye 12

Resting Place 13

Returning Home 14

Expressive Writing 15

Expressive Drawing 22

About the Author 25

Everlasting Love
Helping Teens with Expressions of Loss

ISBN 13: 978-1-7324653-5-0

For information and ordering contact:
Someone Special 2, LLC
Email: someonespecial.joy@gmail.com
Website: someonespecial2.com

Everlasting Love

Words of Encouragement

As a nurse and teacher, even simple knowledge is powerful to positively change both children and adults. Our children are very special and the future of our world. Pure, simple and undefiled knowledge is powerful. Share it, please, because our children need it!

Karen LaFaye Overstreet, RN

Everlasting Love
Helping Teens with Expressions of Loss

STORY BY:
KAREN LAFAYE OVERSTREET, RN

ILLUSTRATIONS BY:
GIANNA JOSEPHINA
&
PETER ISAIAH VALENTE

PUBLISHED BY:
SOMEONE SPECIAL 2, LLC

Dedication

This book is dedicated to my beautiful, precious daughter,
Alysia Danielle Valente and her children Gianna, Peter,
Brielle and Levi.

Special thanks to my grandchildren Gianna
and Peter who loved their mother dearly! They provided
their insight in writing the book and created most of the
illustrations. Through the eyes and mind of children,
adults can accomplish significant things. I love you
Karena, Gianna, Peter, Brielle, Levi, Emry and Jewel.
I specifically want to glorify my Father and his Son
for guiding me every step of the way. Without you,
I cannot do anything! *I love you yesterday,
today and forever!*
Karen L. Overstreet, RN

Introduction

Everlasting Love was designed for teens that
have experienced loss of a family member or friend.
Sometimes life's challenges require some special
adjustments in our families when we experience the loss
of someone very close to us. Although our family member
or friend is no longer with us, their memory can
last forever. The inspiration for this book is to provide
a resource for teens that have experienced the loss
a significant love one and what they may experience
immediately afterwards including their emotions,
support from family, community resources, attending
a funeral and pages to write/draw to express
their feelings.

Most children and teens receive very little
information about the loss of a significant love
one and many adults have confided that they just do
not know what to say to them. **Everlasting Love**
was inspired to provide this service to teens to ensure
they are allowed to express themselves and have
their questions answered too!

Family and Friends

Most families are made up of many members and span over countless generations. Some families are blended and others are brought together through adoption or foster care. What really matters is our love, respect and understanding for each other. There will be times though when events occur that we have no control over such as the loss of a family member or friend.

Illness and Accidents

Sometimes a family member or friend becomes extremely ill or has a terrible accident. They are taken to the hospital. Doctors, nurses and other team members work very hard to make them well again. However, there are conditions or injuries that exceed services provided by medical professionals. Your family member or friend will "pass way" or die. This will significantly impact you, your family and your friend's family too!

Your Feelings

First, you may feel sad or mad
and cry. This is OK because of the love
for your family member or friend. However,
if you feel **very** sad or mad for an
extended period of time, please make
sure you talk to your family, a counselor,
doctor, pastor or friends. It is important
to share your feelings with others.

Saying Good-bye

You, your family and friends may
meet at a special service or funeral to say
good-bye to your family member or friend.
It is OK if you want to say something
special or have a private moment with your
family member or friend. Just let
someone know so this can be arranged
for you. Remember, you can ask
questions and someone will answer
them for you or refer you to someone
who can help!

Resting Place

After you say good-bye, your
special family member or friend
may be taken to their resting place at
the cemetery.   You can come back
to visit your special family member
or friend. Some families bring
flowers to express their love.

.

Returning Home with Family

After leaving the cemetery, you may
meet with others and talk about the
good times you had with your special
family member or friend. There may be
lunch or dinner and music too. If you
have any questions, ask someone, even
if it is many months later. Your love for
your family member or friend will
last forever!

*Remember, during this special
time, expression of your feelings
is important. Please take some time
to write a journal note, or create a
poem, story, or a song about your
special family member or friend. If
you like to express yourself through
a drawing; blank pages are
available, too!

Expressive Writing

Expressive Drawing

Expressive Drawing

Expressive Drawing

About the Author
Karen LaFaye Overstreet, RN, BS

My dedication to serving others began
as a child as I tried to care for baby birds that
had fallen out of their nests. Due to my care
and concern for others, this eventually led to
my career as a Registered Nurse and Teacher.
I love my profession and cannot think of one
day that I did not want to go to work!

My family is very special to me, along
with the importance of striving to do what is
right for others. With two lovely daughters
Karena, Alysia and six grandchildren, Gianna,
Emry, Peter, Jewel, Brielle and Levi, they truly
are a blessing to me. I am very grateful that
Alysia has allowed me and her children to
ensure that other children/teens around the
world will have the opportunity to at least
ask questions, express themselves and have
that "special time" after the loss of a
family member or friend.

Everlasting Love

Yesterday, Today and Forever!

Everlasting Love
Helping Teens with Expressions of Loss

Most children and teens receive
very little information about the loss of a
significant love one and many adults have
confided that they just do not know what
to say to them. **Everlasting Love** was
inspired to provide this service to teens
to ensure they are allowed to express
themselves and have their questions
answered too!

www.someonespecial2.com

www.ingramcontent.com/pod-product-compliance
Lightning Source LLC
Chambersburg PA
CBHW021123020426
42331CB00004B/608